Oscar Wilde

1854–1900

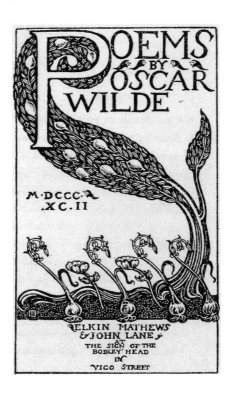

THE SPHINX BY OSCAR WILDE

MELAN CHO LIA

WITH DECORATIONS BY CHARLES RICKETTS
LONDON MDCCCXCIV
ELKIN MATHEWS AND JOHN LANE . AT THE SIGN OF THE BODLEY HEAD.
BOSTON
COPELAND AND DAY LXIX CORNHILL

Oscar Wilde

1854–1900

Sally Brown

THE PIERPONT MORGAN LIBRARY
in association with

THE BRITISH LIBRARY

Published on the occasion of the centenary exhibition, *Oscar Wilde: A Life in Six Acts*, at The British Library, 10 November 2000–4 February 2001, and at The Pierpont Morgan Library, 14 September 2001–13 January 2002.

The exhibition was organised by the British Library. The New York presentation was organised in association with the Morgan Library and sponsored by The Fay Elliott Foundation.

First published 2000 by
The British Library
96 Euston Road
London NW1 2DB

Published 2001 by
The Pierpont Morgan Library
29 East 36th Street
New York, New York 10016

Library of Congress Cataloguing-in-Publication Data
A CIP record is available from The Pierpont Morgan Library.

ISBN 0-87598-134-8

Designed by Julie Rimmer
Printed in England by Balding + Mansell
Frontispiece: Decorated frontispiece for *The Sphinx*, designed by Charles Ricketts.

'The gods had given me almost everything. I had genius, a distinguished name, high social position, brilliancy, intellectual daring: I made art a philosophy and philosophy an art: I altered the minds of men and the colours of things … I awoke the imagination of my century so that it created myth and legend around me.'

Oscar Wilde, De Profundis

Oscar Fingal O'Flahertie Wills Wilde was born in Dublin on 16 October 1854. In later life he dropped all but his first Christian name, explaining that 'A name which is destined to be in everybody's mouth must not be too long. It comes so expensive in advertisements.' His father, William, knighted for his pioneering work with the Irish Censuses, was a doctor, one of the foremost eye and ear surgeons of the day, and a recognised authority on the folklore, natural history and topography of Ireland. His mother, Jane, was a committed Nationalist who wrote inflammatory newspaper articles and poems under the name 'Speranza', and a gifted linguist and translator. They had two other children: William, born in 1852, and Isola, born in 1857. Sir William also had three illegitimate children before his marriage: a son, Henry Wilson, who followed him into medicine, and two daughters, brought up by his clergyman brother, who tragically perished together as young women when their dresses caught fire at a country ball.

Less than a year after Oscar's birth the Wilde family moved from 21 Westland Row, behind Trinity College, Dublin, to a large Georgian house at 1 Merrion Square. As well as six servants, they employed a French maid and a German

Oscar Wilde, aged about two, in a blue velvet dress. (Merlin Holland)

governess, so that the children could be tutored privately, and become fluent in these two languages, in their early years. Although they grew up in comfortable, upper-middle-class professional surroundings, the atmosphere at home was far from conventional. Jane, as eccentric in dress as she was dramatic in manner, became well-known for her weekly salon, or 'conversazione' as she called it, attended by a wide variety of visitors – doctors, lawyers, literary figures, academics – and at which the children were encouraged to mingle with the guests. Sir William Wilde was a distinguished public man, but his private affairs were complicated, at times even scandalous. In 1864 he became embroiled in a disastrous libel case involving one of his patients, a young woman who claimed that he had sexually assaulted her. After this unpleasant episode, his professional life went into decline and he spent increasingly long periods at the family's country house on Lough Corrib.

It was at about this time that Oscar was sent off with his brother Willie to board at the staunchly Protestant Portora Royal School in Elliskillen, which had a superb academic reputation. There he began to excel in Classics and to develop a reputation as a witty conversationalist and story-teller, while studiously avoiding all athletic activities. In 1867 his beloved sister Isola died suddenly, at the age of nine, following a bout of fever; he wrote a poem, 'Requiescat', in her memory, and preserved until his death a lock of her hair in a beautifully decorated envelope crowned with their interlinked initials. At seventeen he won a scholarship to Trinity College, Dublin, where he fell under the spell of one of his tutors, John Pentland Mahaffy, an extremely cultivated man and a remarkable conversationalist; years later, he described him as 'my first and best teacher … the scholar who showed me how to love Greek things'. He flourished during his three years at Trinity, taking up fishing and riding, cultivating his growing interest in art and literature, writing poetry and beating his future court opponent, Edward Carson, to the College's highest honour, a Foundation Scholarship. In 1874 he was awarded the Gold Medal for Greek (later to be pawned and redeemed many times at moments of financial crisis and recovery), and covered himself in glory by winning a Classics

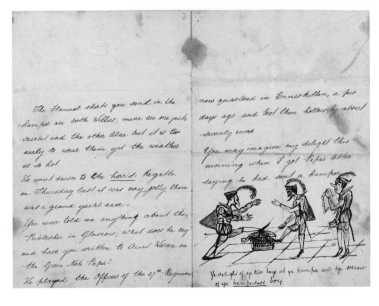

Above: Decorated envelope in which Wilde preserved a lock of his sister Isola's hair. (Merlin Holland)

Left: Part of Wilde's first surviving letter, with a charming illustration, sent from school to his mother on 8 September 1868. (Private Collection)

scholarship, worth ninety-five pounds a year, to Magdalen College, Oxford.

He entered Oxford, which he pronounced the most beautiful city in England, on the day after his twentieth birthday. Magdalen, with its medieval cloisters and deer park, was certainly one of its most beautiful colleges. As well as ancient texts, he studied modern philosophy, philology and history as part of his Classics degree, and his surviving notebooks show how widely read he was in both English and European literature. A fellow undergraduate, writing for the Cornhill Magazine many years later, remembered that he was 'a personality from the first', with his long hair, convulsive laugh, strange swaying gait and abundance of *savoir-faire*. He dressed in the height of Oxford fashion, and took particular care in furnishing his college rooms with portraits of the Pope and Cardinal Manning (symbols of his flirtation with Catholicism), paintings, sculpture, Japanese fans, vases of lilies and a fine collection of blue and white china – which he famously declared he found 'harder to live up to' every day. Several manuscript poems survive from this period, and his letters to two of his closest Magdalen friends, William 'Bouncer' Ward and Reginald 'Kitten' Harding (Wilde himself was known as 'Hosky') give a detailed, witty and fascinating account of University life.

Two Oxford figures who had a deep and lasting influence on Wilde – and, in fact, his whole Oxford generation – were John Ruskin, Slade Professor of Fine Art, and Walter Pater, Fellow of Brasenose College, on whose theories of art and aesthetics he was to base his own flamboyant style. Ruskin, whom Wilde described as 'something of a prophet, a priest and a poet', was a man of high Christian social ideals who believed that art was a vital and essential part of life, not to be enjoyed exclusively by the educated. Pater, whose essays he praised as 'the holy writ of beauty', announced in the Conclusion to his *Studies in the History of the Renaissance* that 'Not the fruit of experience but experience itself is the end', and advocated 'the

On the recent massacres of the Christians in Bulgaria

Christ dost thou live indeed? or are thy bones
Still straightened in their rock-hewn sepulchre?
And do we owe thy rising but to Her
Whose love of thee for all / her sin atones?
For here the air is heavy with men's groans,
The priests that call upon thy name are slain;
Dost thou not hear the bitter wail of pain
From those whose children lie upon the stones?

Our prayers are nought: impenetrable gloom
Covers God's face: and in the star-less night
Over thy Cross the Crescent moon I see.

If thou in very truth didst burst the tomb,
Come down / O Son of Man, and show thy might,
Lest Mahomet be crowned instead of thee.

Oscar Wilde.

Magdalen College.
    Oxford.

Monday.

S· Benedict of Siena ✝

Magdalen College,
Oxford.

Magd. Coll. Tea. Club.

My Dear Bouncer
                    I am very glad
to hear from Mark that
you have come back safe
out of the clutches of
those barbarous Irish – !
was afraid that the
Potatoe–chips   that we live
on over there   would have
been too much for you –
            Some beastly old
Evangelical Parson about
here has, I believe, been
praying for snow – and
his prayers have been quite
            successful – as the

love of art for its own sake'. They appealed to Wilde in different ways: Ruskin to his intellectual and high-minded side, and Pater to his sensual and mystical side. Ruskin's lectures on Florentine aesthetics, which he had attended in his first term, made him eager to visit Italy, with his former tutor Mahaffy, in the summer of 1875; a longer trip with Mahaffy to Rome and Greece, two years later, led to his being fined and 'rusticated' (temporarily sent down) from Magdalen as a punishment for arriving back in college a month late. He went straight to London, where he wrote a review of the opening of the Grosvenor Gallery, his first published piece of prose, before returning to his family in Dublin.

By the time Wilde began his fourth year at Oxford he had suffered the loss of his father, who died – leaving his family in a rather precarious financial condition – in April 1876, two months before his son was awarded a First in Honour Moderations (Greek and Latin language and literature). He had also made the acquaintance of the actress Lillie Langtry, whom he met in his artist friend Frank Miles's studio in London, and had fallen in love with Florence Balcombe, the daughter of an army officer and 'just seventeen with the most perfectly beautiful face I ever saw and not a sixpence of money', as he wrote to his friend Harding from Dublin in August 1876. Wilde gave her a small gold cross with their names inscribed on it, but the romance fizzled out, and Florence went on to become an actress and the wife of Bram Stoker, author of *Dracula*. He spent this year working hard for his final examinations, but found time to enter for the University's annual – and very prestigious – poetry prize, the Newdigate. By great coincidence the subject set for 1878 was 'Ravenna'; he handed in his poem a year to the day after he had visited the city with Mahaffy. On 10 June he learnt that he had won the prize, and on 19 July he was awarded his First in Greats (ancient history and philosophy), the outstanding candidate of his year. 'It is too delightful altogether this display of fireworks at the end of my career' he wrote to

11

RAVENNA.

 A YEAR ago I breathed the Italian air,—
And yet, methinks this northern Spring is fair,—
These fields made golden with the flower of March,
The throstle singing on the feathered larch,
The cawing rooks, the wood-doves fluttering by,
The little clouds that race across the sky;
And fair the violet's gentle drooping head,
The primrose, pale for love uncomforted,
The rose that burgeons on the climbing briar,
The crocus-bed, (that seems a moon of fire
Round-girdled with a purple marriage-ring);
And all the flowers of our English Spring,
Fond snow-drops, and the bright-starred daffodil.
Up starts the lark beside the murmuring mill,
And breaks the gossamer-threads of early dew;
And down the river, like a flame of blue,
Keen as an arrow flies the water-king,
While the brown linnets in the greenwood sing.
A year ago!—it seems a little time
Since last I saw that lordly southern clime,
Where flower and fruit to purple radiance blow,
And like bright lamps the fabled apples glow.

*The first page of Wilde's
Newdigate Prize poem,
'Ravenna', published in
Oxford 1878.
(BL C.131.d.19)*

Ward, adding that 'The dons are "astonied" beyond words – the Bad Boy doing so well in the end!' His mother was ecstatic: 'Well, after all, we have a Genius … This gives you a certainty of success in the future – You can now trust your own intellect, and know what it can do.'

Wilde could not live on genius alone, and despite his spectacular academic success, Magdalen did not offer him a Fellowship. Ward later remembered his friend's defiant – and prescient – response: 'I won't be a dried up old don, anyhow. I'll be a poet, a writer, a dramatist. Somehow or other I'll be famous, and if not famous, I'll be notorious.' He set his sights on London and went to live with Frank Miles in his 'untidy and romantic' house in Salisbury Street, off the Strand. They set about decorating it in high aesthetic style, with white panelling, Greek rugs and hangings, tiles from Damascus, and drawings by Burne-Jones. Wilde's legacy from his father was soon diminished by their increasingly extravagant way of life.

Miles was already well-established in London society as a sketcher of the great and the beautiful, and it was through him that Wilde met the leading actresses and 'Professional Beauties' of the day: Ellen Terry, Sarah Bernhardt (in London with the Comédie-Française) and, once again, Lillie Langtry. He attended their first nights and supper parties, praised and flattered them at every opportunity, published sonnets to them – and in Lillie Langtry's case, took her to lectures and tutored her in Latin. They in their turn were captivated by him – his wit, his extraordinary charm and his melodious voice, once described as 'the texture of brown velvet played like a cello'. As his social status rose, the Prince of Wales himself pronounced that 'Not to know Mr Wilde is not to be known.'

Amidst all this adulation, Wilde was becoming conscious of his lack of literary progress; poetic tributes to actresses ('Lily of love, pure and inviolate!/Tower of ivory! Red rose of fire!') gave way to more sustained work, and by the autumn of 1880 his first play, *Vera; or The Nihilists* – based on the assassination of the Governor of St Petersburg by a young Russian woman in 1878 – was finished and privately printed. By March 1881 its subject had become unexpectedly topical through the murder of Czar Alexander II, and its première was scheduled for December, only to be halted by the assassination in America of President Garfield six months later. (In the end, *Vera* was produced in New York in August 1883, where it was slated by the critics – the *New York Herald* called it 'long-drawn dramatic rot' – and closed after a week.) In April 1881 – now living with Frank Miles in a considerably more expensive house in the newly fashionable Tite Street in Chelsea – Wilde wrote to a publisher: 'I am anxious to publish a volume of poems immediately … Possibly my name needs no introduction.'

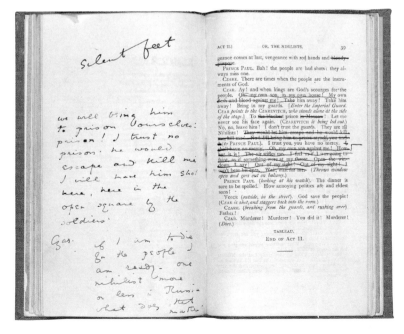

A rare copy of Vera, *annotated by Wilde, privately published in New York, 1882. (BL C.60.k.8)*

Published by David Bogue but at the author's expense, 750 copies of a volume simply entitled *Poems*, printed on hand-made paper, came out in July, to a mixed critical reception. *Punch* dismissed its contents as 'Swinburne and water', while the *Saturday Review* declared that it was 'marred everywhere by imitation, insincerity and bad taste'. Undeterred, Wilde sent copies to all his acquaintances of note, including Swinburne himself, the Prime Minister

THE JUDGE

A THING OF BEAUTY NOT A JOY FOREVER.
Rise and Fall of a "Vera" Wilde Æsthete.

Illustration from The Judge, *1883, showing 'The Rise and Fall of a "Vera" Wilde Æsthete'. (BL PP 6383)*

William Gladstone, Robert Browning and Matthew Arnold, who praised its 'true feeling for rhythm … which is at the bottom of all success in poetry'. A copy was requested by the Oxford Union, only to be returned, with some embarrassment, after an undergraduate, Oliver Elton, denounced its contents as thin, immoral and derivative, and moved that the volume should not be accepted. (The rejected copy still survives as an important and rather poignant collector's item.) Another unhappy consequence of the publication of these poems was the reaction of Frank Miles's clergyman father, who considered them sinful and disturbing; he persuaded his son to drop Wilde, who was unceremoniously forced to move out of the Tite Street house into furnished rooms.

Meanwhile, the burgeoning aesthetic movement – or 'craze' as its detractors called it – had become familiar to London society by the early 1880s, and cartoons of ' aesthetic types' by George du Maurier began to appear in *Punch*. These included a character with flowing locks and a passion for blue china called, variously, Oscuro Wildgoose, the Wilde-eyed poet and Ossian Wilderness. Such exposure only served to fuel Wilde's campaign of self-promotion. In the spring of 1881 a new Gilbert and Sullivan opera, *Patience*, opened at the London Opéra Comique. Its main characters were Reginald Bunthorne, a 'fleshly poet', and Archibald Grosvenor, an

In the Gold Room.
a Harmony.

_____

Her ivory hands on the ivory keys
    Strayed in a fitful fantasy,
Like the silver gleam when the poplar trees
    Rustle their pale leaves listlessly,
Or like the drifting foam of a restless sea
When the waves show their teeth in the flying breeze.

Her gold hair fell on the wall of gold
    Like the delicate gossamer tangles spun
On the burnished disk of the marigold,
    Or the sun-flower turning to meet the sun
When the gloom of the jealous night is done,
And the spear of the lily is aureoled.

And her sweet red lips on these lips of mine
    Burned like the ruby fire set
In the swinging lamp of a crimson shrine,
    Or the bleeding wounds of the pomegranate,
    Or the heart of the lotos drenched and wet
With the spilt-out blood of the rose-red wine.

Autograph draft of Wilde's poem 'In the Gold Room', published in Poems, *1881. (BL Zweig MS 199, f.1)*

'idyllic poet', each representing different aspects of well-known aesthetes, who included Swinburne, the artists Whistler and Rossetti – and, most notably, Wilde himself. Following the success of *Patience* in London, its producer, D'Oyly Carte, took it to New York in September 1881. A North American tour was planned for the following year, and Wilde – eager to make an international reputation, and also to earn some much-needed money – accepted an invitation to deliver a series of lectures which would give the Americans a taste of real-life aestheticism. By December, all financial matters had been settled and he prepared himself for this new part by ordering some suitably aesthetic outfits and a long, heavy, fur-lined green overcoat to which he became deeply attached, later writing that 'it was all over America with me … it knows me perfectly'. It enfolded him when he set sail for New York on Christmas Eve, without a word of a lecture written.

Photograph of Wilde in New York by Napoleon Sarony, January 1882. (Library of Congress)

From the moment of his much-quoted statement to a customs official on his arrival at the New York docks that 'I have nothing to declare but my genius', Wilde's every move and pronouncement was eagerly reported by the press. Asked to give a definition of aestheticism, he described it as 'a search after the signs of the beautiful … to speak more exactly, the search after the secret of life' – a reply, as one listener remarked, 'suggesting that there would be much to be made clear in his forthcoming lectures'. Expecting a limp-wristed, pale and delicate creature, the crowd of waiting reporters was surprised by his robust appearance; the *New York Times* commented that 'The most striking thing … is his height, which is several inches over six feet, and the next thing to attract attention is his hair, which is of dark brown colour, and falls down upon his shoulders … Instead of having a small delicate hand fit only to caress a lily, his fingers are long and when doubled up would hit a hard knock ...' Another journalist remarked on his 'sing-song' voice, its 'great peculiarity being a rhythmic chant in which every fourth syllable is accentuated'.

One of the first things Wilde did in New York was to take himself off to be photographed by the exotically named Napoleon Sarony, one of the foremost photographers of the day, in a variety of aesthetic poses and outfits. The manager of his lecture tour, Colonel Morse, was shrewd enough to waive the large fee photographers usually had to pay in order to take photographs of celebrities. Despite the social demands immediately made upon him, Wilde managed to write his lecture, entitled 'The English Renaissance' – a disquisition on the school of creative art as practised by Whistler and Rossetti and the decorative arts movement as championed by Ruskin and William Morris – in time for his first appearance at the Chickering Hall, resplendent in a 'dark purple sack-coat and knee-breeches', on 9 January. Its text was soon shortened and recast as 'The Decorative Arts'; a reserve lecture, 'The House Beautiful', was written during a week's break in Chicago.

Such was the success of these lectures, which took Wilde from the eastern seaboard to Canada and the furthest reaches of California, dazzling his audiences (which included a group of hard-drinking miners in Colorado) with his flamboyant outfits and his artistic views, that the proposed four month tour eventually stretched to nearly a year. 'Aesthetic' images of him – many produced illicitly – were to be seen everywhere, from department store trade-cards to musical scores and advertisements for cowboy boots; pirated editions of his works appeared, and he was caricatured in innumerable periodicals.

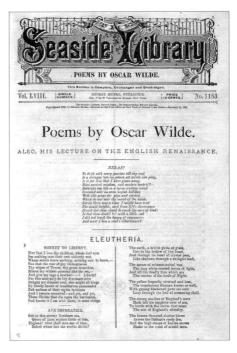

Piracy of Wilde's Poems by the Seaside Library, New York, 19 January 1882. (BL 11651.m.63)

Between lectures, he was, as he wrote to a friend, 'torn to bits by society. Immense receptions, wonderful dinners, crowds wait for my carriage. I wave a gloved hand and an ivory cane and they cheer … Rooms are hung with white lilies for me everywhere.' He also made private visits to such literary lions as the poets Longfellow and Whitman, who described him to the press as 'frank, outspoken and manly'. More importantly, he arranged for *Vera* to be staged in New York the following year and was commissioned to write a blank-verse tragedy, *The Duchess of Padua*, for the actress Mary Anderson. When he returned home at the end of December with more than £1,200 in his pocket, he could congratulate himself on having carried out his mission to 'civilise America' by the moral inspiration of beauty.

Above and below: Original designs by Charles Ricketts for the covers of Wilde's Poems, *1892, and* The Sphinx', *1894. (Add. MS 37942, ff. 10, 14).*

Speranza, now living in London, had written excitedly to her son in September 1882, 'I think you will be mobbed when you come back by eager crowds and be obliged to shelter in cabs.' Wilde, however, had been longing 'to get back to real literary work', and a month after his return took himself off to Paris to write his play, which was due by the end of March. He arrived bearing letters of introduction and several presentation copies of his *Poems* and installed himself in the Hotel Voltaire, on the Left Bank. From there he launched himself into Parisian literary life, aping Balzac with his white dressing-gown and socialising with many of the foremost literary figures of the period, including Edmond de Goncourt (who described him rather dismissively as being *'au sexe douteux'*), Victor Hugo (who fell asleep after exchanging a few words with him) and Paul Verlaine (who took umbrage at Wilde's failure to ply him with enough absinthe when they met in the Café Vachette). He also developed a friendship with Robert Sherard, an English journalist who was to be

his first biographer. Amidst all this, he resumed work on 'The Sphinx', a rich and sonorous poem on the subject of the *femme fatale* which he had begun at Oxford, and managed to finish *The Duchess of Padua* and send it off to Mary Anderson by the end of March. In the event, she turned it down, much to his chagrin: apart from his dramatic ambitions, he had been living on the expectation of the $4,000 which was to be paid on its acceptance. The play was eventually performed in New York in 1893, but, sadly, to no better a critical reception than *Vera* had received ten years earlier.

On Wilde's return from Paris, he embarked on a British lecture tour, civilising the provinces with a new subject, 'Personal Impressions of America', in his repertoire. It was on a lecture visit to Dublin in November 1883 that he proposed to Constance Lloyd, four years younger than him and the daughter of a barrister, who had died when she was sixteen. She had been living with her grandfather in London when

Page from the autograph manuscript of The Duchess of Padua.
(Collection of Fay and Geoffrey Elliott)

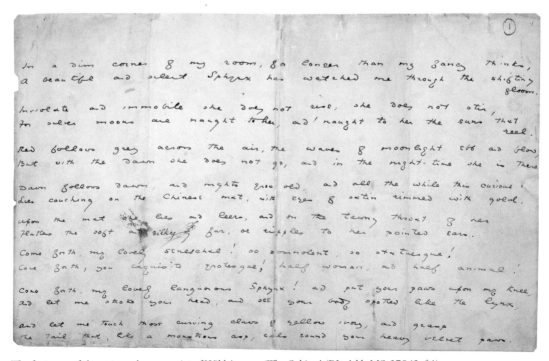

The first page of the autograph manuscript of Wilde's poem 'The Sphinx' (BL Add. MS 37942, f.1).

Constance Wilde in 1892. (Merlin Holland)

they had first met in May 1881. Constance was very attractive, well-educated, interested in art and music, a good linguist and an aspiring writer; her earliest surviving letter to Wilde discusses the merits of *Vera*. Wilde described her to a friend as 'a grave, slight, violet-eyed little Artemis'. They were married in London at St James's Church, Sussex Gardens, on 29 May 1884, Constance in a suitably aesthetic dress of 'rich creamy satin' with a high Medici collar and a silver girdle around her waist. Following a honeymoon in Dieppe and Paris, during which Wilde spent some of his time roaming the city with Sherard, the couple returned to London. They had taken a lease on their own 'House Beautiful' at 16 Tite Street, a few doors away from where Wilde had lived with Frank Miles three years earlier. Its elaborate interior decoration, with a spectacular dining room in white blended with pale blue and yellow, a ground-floor library decorated in Moorish style, and a second-floor drawing room with peacock feathers adorning its ceiling, was entrusted to the designer and architect Edward Godwin. Here they settled down to married life, entertaining at home and going out together in society. Their letters to each other at this time reveal their deep mutual love and happiness, and they both took great pleasure in their two sons: Cyril, born in June 1885 and Vyvyan, born in November 1886.

As a family man with no regular income, Wilde needed to make more money than he was receiving from occasional lectures and reviews, largely for the *Pall Mall Gazette*. 'Believe me that it is impossible to live by literature', he wrote in a letter of 1885. 'By journalism one may make an income, but rarely by pure literary work ....' It was not until the spring of 1887 that the chance of a regular income arose: Thomas Wemyss Reid, the general manager of Cassell's publishing house and an admirer of Wilde's journalism, offered him the editorship of a new monthly publication, *The Lady's World*,

Above: Letter to Wilde from Constance Lloyd, written in late 1883 or early 1884. (Private Collection)

Below: Letter sent from Wilde to Constance on 16 December 1884, six months after their marriage. (Pierpont Morgan Library)

*Above: Cyril Wilde, aged six.
(Merlin Holland)*

*Below: Vyvyan Wilde, aged
five.(Merlin Holland)*

subtitled a 'Magazine of Fashion and Society' and badly in need of revitalisation. Realising that this presented the perfect opportunity to launch himself back into the public eye, Wilde accepted with alacrity, writing to Reid: 'We should take a wider range, and deal not merely with what women wear, but what they feel. *The Lady's World* should be made the recognised organ for the expression of women's opinions on all subjects of literature, art and modern life …' He persuaded Cassell's to change the title to *The Woman's World* ('The present name … has a certain taint of vulgarity about it'), and spent the next few months preparing the ground for his editorship, which began in November. The first issue had a new masthead, a redesigned cover and Wilde's name on the title page; he managed to attract a range of talented writers, including his mother and his wife, although Queen Victoria firmly declined his request for a poem.

The relaunched magazine was a success at first, and Wilde an energetic and assiduous editor; his assistant, Arthur Fish, pronounced him 'extraordinary', while perceptively describing his editorship as 'Pegasus in harness'. Routine did not suit Wilde's temperament; 'I have known men come to London full of bright prospects and seen them complete wrecks in a few months through the habit of answering letters', he informed Fish. Inevitably, the monotony of commuting by underground train and on foot to the magazine's office in Ludgate Hill from Sloane Square three days a week took its toll, and his commitment to this new role gradually dwindled – as did the magazine's circulation – until he left in October 1889. Nevertheless, the experience had re-established him as a leading writer, relieved some of his financial pressures and primed him for the next, hugely creative period of his life, as stories inspired by the tales and legends of his childhood in Ireland – 'a Celtic world dominated by ghosts and God', as another Irishman described it – began to pour out of him. Folklore and the supernatural imbue *The Canterville Ghost, Lord Arthur*

Savile's Crime and his first collection of short stories, *The Happy Prince and Other Tales* (written, he always insisted, 'not for children but for childlike people from eighteen to eighty'), published in May 1888. His brilliant essay 'The Decay of Lying', in which he made a plea for more imagination to counteract the growing influence of excessive realism in literature, appeared in 1889: 'I have blown my trumpet against the gate of dullness' he wrote to a friend on its publication. In the following year, *The Picture of Dorian Gray* was published in its original form in the American *Lippincott's Monthly Magazine*.

This dark and disturbing piece of writing was described by Wilde as the story of 'a young man selling his soul in exchange for eternal youth – an idea that is old in the history of literature, but to which I have given new form'. He predicted that it would ultimately be recognised as 'a real work of art with a strong ethical message in it', but as soon as it appeared in print the response of the press was almost universally hostile. *The Daily Mail* condemned it as 'a tale spawned from the leprous literature of the French *décadents* – a poisonous book … heavy with the odours of moral and spiritual putrefaction', while the *Scots Observer*, though conceding that its author had 'brains, and art, and style', warned that 'if he can write for none but outlawed noblemen and telegraph boys, the sooner he takes to tailoring (or some other decent trade) the better for his own reputation and public morals.' The mention of noblemen and telegraph boys was a reference to the recent (and hushed-up) Cleveland Street scandal, in which various aristocrats were discovered to be frequenting a homosexual brothel serviced by boys from the nearby General Post Office.

Constance is said to have remarked: 'Since *Dorian Gray*, no-one will speak to us.' It was once described as the only French novel written in English – and it is certainly true that Wilde's fascination with the decadent atmosphere of *fin-de-siècle* Paris had partly inspired it. Of the deluge of criticism from

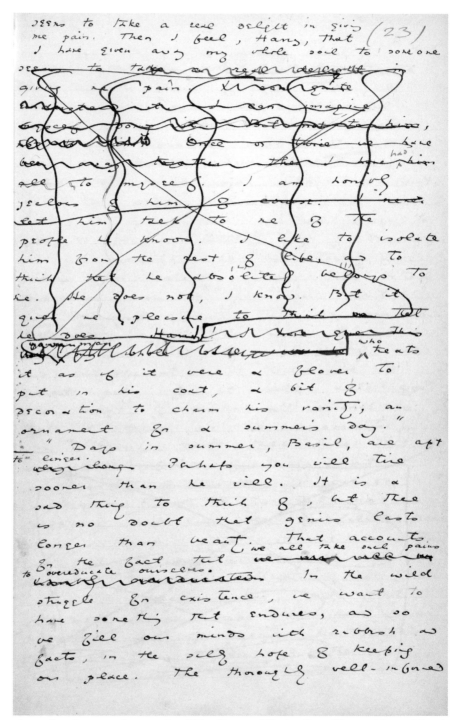

A page from the autograph manuscript of The Picture of Dorian Gray. *(Pierpont Morgan Library)*

the press, he wrote that it made him 'despair of the possibility of any general culture in England … there is not a single literary critic in France of high standing who would think for a moment of criticising it from an ethical standpoint'. In late 1891 he went back to Paris to work on his new play, written in French, a re-telling of the dramatic and disturbing story of Salomé, the Judean princess who danced before King Herod and was rewarded with the severed head of John the Baptist on a platter. André Gide, who met Wilde at this time, recalled that he radiated 'the chief gift of great men: success. His gesture, his look triumphed … His books astonished, charmed … no sooner did he arrive, than his name ran from mouth to mouth ….' Six months after he left Paris, Sarah Bernhardt, then fifty, had been persuaded to take the title role of the sixteen-year-old Salomé; rehearsals had already begun in London when the Lord Chamberlain, official censor of plays, refused to grant a licence, citing an old and obscure law prohibiting the representation of Biblical figures on the stage.

Aubrey Beardsley's illustration for Salomé*, with a caricature of Wilde in the bottom right-hand corner.*
(BL C.129.d.12)

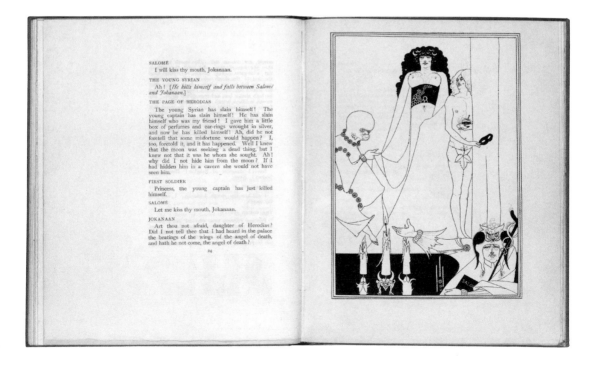

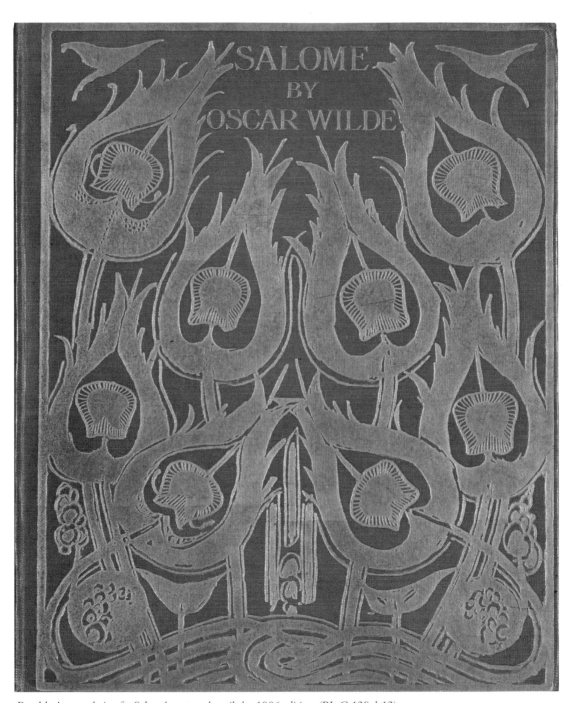

Beardsley's cover design for Salomé, *not used until the 1906 edition. (BL C.129.d.12)*

Both Wilde – who threatened to leave England – and Bernhardt, who had taken the Palace Theatre for a season, were incensed, but powerless to act further: the play's heady atmosphere of decadence and eroticism, with a disturbing hint of necrophilia, was too strong for English sensibilities.

Meanwhile, although his affection for his wife and two young sons never left him, Wilde's personal life was taking a new turn with his growing awareness – or acceptance – of his homosexuality, and the need to conceal it. Apart from any other considerations, it was a dangerous position to be in at this time, since the 1885 Criminal Law Amendment Act had made same-sex relations between men punishable by imprisonment. In 1884 he had written to a young Cambridge undergraduate: 'I myself would sacrifice everything for a new experience ... There is an unknown land full of strange flowers and subtle perfumes, a land of which it is a joy of all joys to dream, a land where all things are perfect and poisonous.' Three years later, a young Canadian, Robert Ross – who was to remain one of his most loyal and devoted friends and manage his literary estate after his death – came to stay at Tite Street, and almost certainly became Wilde's first homosexual lover. This brief affair was followed by dalliances with others, including the poets Richard Le Gallienne (to whom Wilde wrote, 'I hope the laurels are not too thick across your brow for me to kiss your eyelids') and John Gray, who later became a Catholic priest. It was in the summer of 1891 that he first met Lord Alfred 'Bosie' Douglas, introduced to him by another young poet, Lionel Johnson.

A golden-haired, alabaster-pale, extremely attractive but arrogant and wilful young man of twenty-one (sixteen years younger than Wilde), Douglas was an undergraduate at Magdalen College, Oxford, reading Classics and editor of *The Spirit Lamp*, 'An Aesthetic, Literary and Critical Magazine'. The third and youngest son of the violent and erratic Ninth Marquess of Queensberry (author of the Queensberry rules for boxing), he had poetic ambitions and claimed to have read *Dorian Gray* at least nine times. They saw each other only occasionally at first, but in early 1892 events brought them into closer contact when Douglas, anxious and distraught, came to Wilde for help over an indiscreet letter with which he was being blackmailed. Soon after this, they became lovers; Wilde rapidly became infatuated with his 'gilt-mailed boy', writing to a friend, 'He lies like a hyacinth on the sofa and I worship him.' He showered Douglas with telegrams, letters, gifts, champagne, lavish dinners at the Savoy, boxes at the theatre; Douglas in turn became captivated by the magical quality of Wilde's conversation, his brilliance and charm. Their relationship eclipsed all Wilde's earlier passions, but its intensity was often painful and exhausting. In a letter of March 1893 he begged Douglas not to 'make scenes' with him: 'They kill me, they wreck the loveliness of life.'

At this period, Wilde was often absent from the family house in Tite Street, taking chambers in St James's, ostensibly in order to write, and staying in various hotels. It was Douglas who drew him deeper into the homosexual underworld of London, with its 'renters', or male prostitutes; in a letter written a few years later, he confessed that 'so far from his leading me astray it was I that (unwittingly) pushed him over the precipice'. Wilde was fascinated by what he found there, delighting in the company of these boys: 'It was like feasting with panthers. The danger was half the excitement … They were to me the brightest of gilded snakes. Their poison was part of their perfection.' He was spending far too much money at this time – Douglas was recklessly extravagant – and so it was fortunate that the actor-manager George Alexander had commissioned him to write a contemporary play (having turned down *The Duchess of Padua*) when he took over the management of the St James's Theatre.

Lady Windermere's Fan, subtitled 'A Play about a Good Woman', opened, to huge acclaim, in February 1892. Its brilliantly witty repartee and smart society setting were subtly used to highlight hypocrisy as well as the nature of goodness.

Photograph of Wilde and Alfred Douglas at Oxford, probably taken in May 1893. (Private Collection)

Wilde attended many of the rehearsals and argued with Alexander about various effects, particularly the 'element of suspense and curiosity, so essentially dramatic'. Alexander had offered him £1,000 for the rights but he insisted on a percentage of the profits, and as a result made £7,000 in the first year of the play's production. Constance was in the audience for the first night, as were Florence Balcombe (now Mrs Stoker), Lillie Langtry, Robert Ross, Douglas and Edward Shelley, a publishers' clerk with whom Wilde was then involved. The playwright strode onto the stage as the final curtain fell, smoking a cigarette, and acknowledged the audience's cheers with a short speech congratulating them on their intelligence and the 'great success' of their performance, 'which persuades me that you think almost as highly of the play as I do myself'. Frank Harris, editor of the *Fortnightly Review*, wrote that Wilde had 'at last come into his kingdom'.

The play ran for 156 performances and went on tour in the provinces. Wilde seemed to have found his true literary medium and in quick succession wrote *A Woman of No Importance* (1892), *An Ideal Husband* (1893) and his comic masterpiece, *The Importance of Being Earnest* (1894), all along fairly similar lines, displaying a brilliant command of dialogue, and playing on themes of concealment and revelation, with an underlying moral lightly sketched in. Speranza was kept very busy collecting all her son's press notices, but wrote to warn him that now he had made his name and 'taken a distinguished place in the circle of intellects' he must also take care of his health and 'keep clear of suppers and late nights and champagne'. On one such occasion, a party held after the opening of *A Woman of No Importance*, Wilde was disturbed by another warning, from a palmist who predicted that he would 'send himself into exile'. As his relationship with Douglas, stormy from the first, became more complicated and fraught, with many painful quarrels and emotional reconciliations – 'My fault', as he later wrote, 'was not that I did not part from you, but that I parted

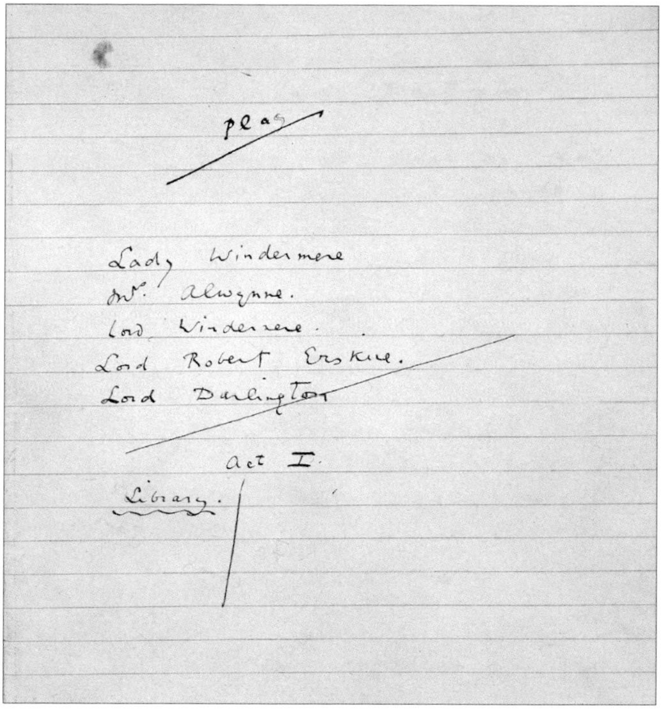

pleas

Lady Windermere
Mrs. Alwynne.
Lord Windermere.
Lord Robert Erskine.
Lord Darlington

Act I.

Library.

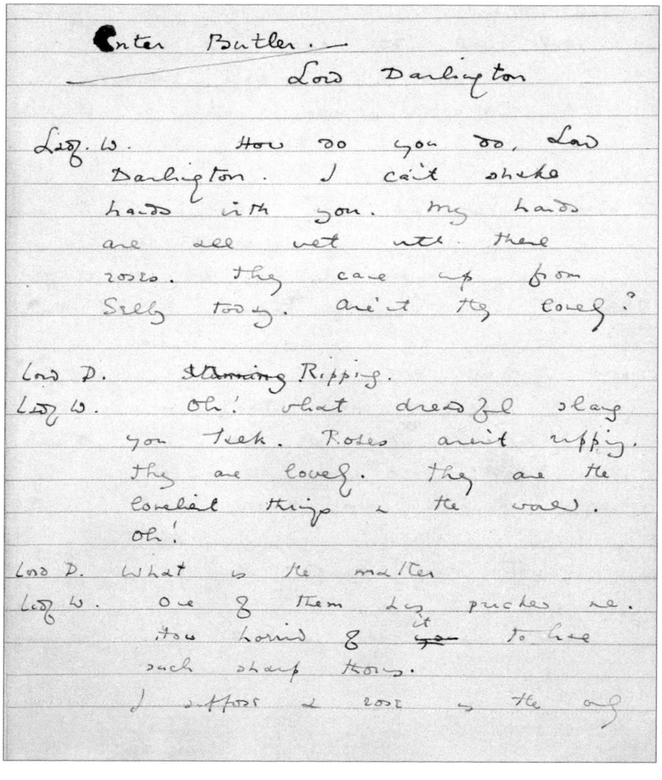

Enter Butler.
Lord Darlington

Lady W.   How do you do, Lord
Darlington. I can't shake
hands with you. My hands
are all wet with these
roses. They came up from
Selby today. aren't they lovely?

Lord D.   Stunning Ripping.
Lady W.   Oh! what dreadful slang
you talk. Roses aren't ripping.
they are lovely. They are the
loveliest things in the world.
Oh!
Lord D.   What is the matter
Lady W.   One of them has pricked me.
how horrid of it to have
such sharp thorns.
I suppose a rose is the only

*The first two pages of the
autograph manuscript of
Lady Windermere's Fan.
(BL Add. MS 37943, ff. 1, 2)*

from you far too often' – he was also plagued by the 'vulture creditors' circling round him as he continued to spend far more than he earned.

One crisis rapidly followed another, and events began to take on an ominous momentum. Wilde survived a blackmail attempt over love letters he had sent to Douglas, only to be followed all over London by the Marquess of Queensberry, full of outrage at their 'loathsome and disgusting' relationship and his son's defiantly scornful attitude towards him. At the end of June 1894, he called on Wilde in Tite Street, furious and abusive, vowing to thrash him if he ever found him again in a public restaurant with Bosie – to which Wilde famously replied, 'I do not know what the Queensberry rules are, but the Oscar Wilde rule is to shoot on sight.' 'It is intolerable' he wrote two months later, 'to be dogged by a maniac.' In October Queensberry's heir, Viscount Drumlangrig, was killed in what was reported as a shooting accident but was probably suicide: there was suspicion that he was being blackmailed over a relationship with Lord Rosebery, now

The 'handbag scene' from the autograph manuscript of The Importance of Being Earnest, *with the formidable Lady Bracknell here called Lady Brancaster.*
(BL Add. MS 37948, ff.109v–110)

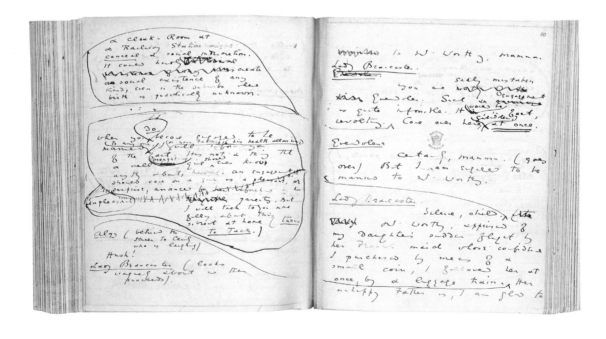

Prime Minister. Having lost one son to what he saw as the evils of homosexuality, Queensberry was more distressed and incensed than ever about Bosie's relationship with Wilde.

After the hugely successful opening of *An Ideal Husband* at the Haymarket Theatre (with the Prince of Wales in the royal box) in early January 1895, Wilde and Douglas went off for a holiday in Algiers. Hearing of this, Queensberry planned to create a dramatic disturbance at the opening night of *The Importance of Being Earnest* on 14 February, by presenting Wilde with a grotesque bouquet of vegetables. In the event, the police were alerted to this potential threat to public order, and the Marquess was denied entry to the St James's Theatre, only to pace furiously outside in the worst snowstorm London had experienced for several years. Four days later, he strode into Wilde's club, the Albemarle, and left his card with the hall porter: written on it, in his terrible scrawl, was the misspelt message, 'For Oscar Wilde, posing somdomite'. When Wilde found this waiting for him, some days later, he immediately sent off an agitated note to Robert Ross: 'Bosie's father has left a card at my club with hideous words on it. I don't see anything now but a criminal prosecution. My whole life seems ruined by this man … I don't know what to do.' What he did was to sue Queensberry for criminal libel. As he later put in *De Profundis*, his long prison letter to Douglas: 'I was no longer the Captain of my soul and did not know it. I allowed you to dominate me and your father to frighten me. I saw no possible escape from either of you. Blindly I staggered as an ox into the shambles.'

In suing Queensberry, Wilde must have been been aware that he would have to defend in court his relationship with Douglas and possibly also his public behaviour and published works; but he could not have anticipated the explosive evidence which the Marquess's lawyers extracted from the homosexual underworld, some of which was disclosed to him in Queensberry's 'Plea of Justification' shortly before the trial opened. At this point he might have

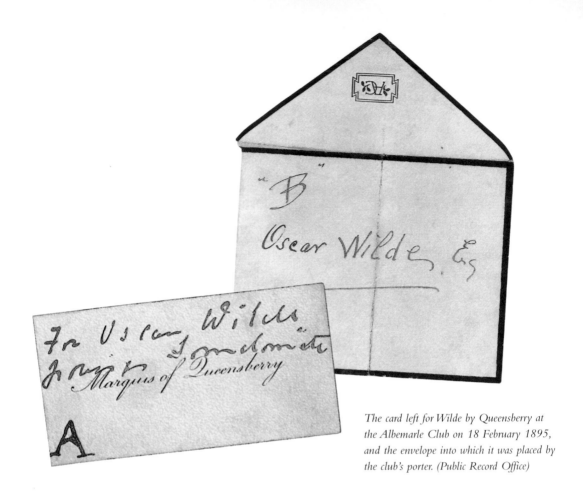

The card left for Wilde by Queensberry at the Albemarle Club on 18 February 1895, and the envelope into which it was placed by the club's porter. (Public Record Office)

withdrawn, and several of his friends urged him to do so, but still he chose to see the play out, and the trial of Wilde versus Queensberry opened at the Old Bailey on the morning of 3 April 1895. Wilde was represented by Sir Edward Clarke, then Solicitor General; Edward Carson, his former Trinity College contemporary, was Queensberry's counsel. Arriving in some style in a carriage and pair, Wilde strolled calmly into the courtroom. He acquitted himself well at first, eloquently and wittily defending his views on art and morality in relation to *Dorian Gray*; when questioned about the only sentence he had judged it prudent to omit from the published book, 'Have you ever adored a young man madly?', he replied, 'No, not madly. I prefer love – it is a higher form. I have never given adoration to anybody but myself.' Carson was – or so it seemed – unable to make much significant headway, and Wilde left the court believing that he would win the case.

On the second day, matters did not go so well. Wilde was over-confident, Carson more determined and cunning, listing the names and occupations of the 'homeless and shiftless boys' Wilde was alleged to have consorted with, and laying subtle traps which he fell into several times. When asked if he had ever kissed a boy who had been Douglas's servant at Oxford, his reply was 'Oh dear no. He was a peculiarly plain boy. I pitied him for it.' When, on the third day, it was made clear that Carson was about to produce a clutch of witnesses ready to give explicit evidence about their relationships with Wilde, Clarke immediately advised him to withdraw from his suit, and the jury was ordered to return a 'not guilty' verdict. Queensberry's solicitor lost no time in sending all the trial papers, including the statements of the witnesses who had not been called, to the Director of Public Prosecutions. The next stage, the prosecution of Wilde for homosexual offences, was inevitable; he had just enough time to escape to France, but with a characteristic mixture of bravery and fatalism chose not to do so, and was arrested that evening at the Cadogan Hotel. He spent the night in a cell at Bow Street Police Station; the following morning, he was charged with offences under the 1885 Criminal Law Amendment Act and, with bail refused, transferred to Holloway Prison, where he remained until his first trial against the Crown began three weeks later. Douglas, who had visited him nearly every day in Holloway – 'A slim thing, gold-haired like an angel, stands always at my side' – left London for the Continent on the day before it opened, persuaded by Clarke and others that his presence in London would do Wilde's case no good.

From the moment of Wilde's arrest, events moved with a terrible swiftness. All his books in print were removed from sale; his name was expunged from the programmes and posters advertising his plays; his wife and children went into hiding; and, to his great anguish, the bailiffs moved into his Tite Street house: 'All my charming things are to be sold: my

Burne-Jones drawings ... my china; my library with its collection of presentation volumes from almost every poet of my time ... its beautifully bound editions of my father's and mother's works.' After several gruelling preliminary hearings at Bow Street, on 26 April he found himself once again in the dock at the Old Bailey, charged with twenty-five acts of 'gross indecency'. Sir Edward Clarke continued to represent him, generously waiving his fee. Various boys, who had been pressurised into appearing in order to escape prosecution themselves, were called to give graphic testimony against him; when he took the stand he denied all charges of indecency, claiming to be merely 'a lover of youth'. His finest moment came when Douglas's poem 'Two Loves' was read aloud: he responded with an extremely eloquent and moving defence of the love between men 'that dare not speak its name', drawing applause from the gallery.

The highly publicised trial, which lasted five days, ended with a hung jury. Released on bail, Wilde found that no London hotel would take him in, and eventually he took refuge with an old friend, Ada Leverson, at her Kensington house. Again, his friends – joined by his wife – urged him to flee the country, and again he refused, writing to Douglas: 'I decided that it was nobler and more beautiful to stay ... I did not want to be a called a coward or a deserter. A false name, a disguise, a hunted life, all that is not for me ...'. A re-trial opened on 20 May, and lasted six days, with yet more evidence, some offered by staff from the Savoy Hotel. In his final speech, Clarke laid stress on the tainted nature of the witnesses and their statements, declaring that the trial was 'operating as an act of indemnity for all the blackmailers in London'; Wilde described the prosecution's summing-up as 'appalling ... like a passage from Dante'. This time, the jury was unanimous in convicting him. In passing a sentence of two years' hard labour – the maximum allowed by law – the judge proclaimed that the defendant had clearly been 'at the centre of a circle of extensive corruption of the most hideous kind' and that this had been the worst case he had ever tried. Wilde was sent briefly to Holloway and then to Pentonville Prison; Constance, who had sent their sons away to safety in Switzerland, stayed on until this point, when she too went abroad.

Wilde's first six months in prison were spent in Pentonville and Wandsworth, which he described as 'not fit for dogs'. His hair was cut short and he was issued with the standard prison uniform. At Pentonville his cell was thirteen feet long, seven feet wide and nine high, and he slept on a plank bed with no mattress. After a medical examination he was passed as being fit for light labour, which involved tasks such as oakum picking (shredding hard rope into fibre by hand) and sewing mailbags, as well as time spent on the treadmill. He was kept in solitary confinement, apart from the daily hour's exercise with other inmates in the prison yard, during which talking was forbidden. The prison food was meagre and bad, and his health quickly deteriorated. At first, the only books he was allowed were a Bible, prayer book and hymn book; later he was allowed one book a week from the prison library, and R.B Haldane, a member of the Prison Commission, arranged for him to be provided with further works of his own choice, which included St Augustine, Newman and Pater. For the first three months he was not allowed to communicate with the outside world; thereafter he was allowed to write and receive one letter, and to receive a visit from behind a wire screen from up to three

'Closing Scene at the Old Bailey' from The Illustrated Police News *of 4 May 1895. (BL Newspaper Library)*

people, every three months. His first visitor was Sherard, who found him 'greatly depressed'; when Constance visited him, she was shocked and horrified at his surroundings and physical condition: 'I could not see him and I could not touch him. I scarcely spoke.'

In November, unable to pay the legal fees incurred by Queensberry in his libel trial (which Douglas had originally promised his brother would settle), Wilde was declared bankrupt; later that month, he was transferred to Reading Gaol, a humiliating and traumatic journey which took place by public transport and during which he was jeered at while waiting, handcuffed and in prison clothes, to change trains at Clapham Junction. In February 1896 his mother died. Constance – who had been forced to revert to an old family name, Holland, in order to protect herself and her sons from gossip and hostility – travelled from Genoa, where she was then living, in order to break the news to him. It was the last time they were to see each other. Financial arrangements were made which led finally to her settling £150 a year on her husband, provided that he did not 'notoriously consort with evil or disreputable persons'. In July, Wilde sent his first petition to the Home Secretary, requesting a mitigation of his sentence; this was refused, but the Prison Commissioners did give permission for extra books and writing materials to be provided. In January 1897, encouraged by the new Governor at Reading, Major Nelson, under whose enlightened regime his health and mental outlook started to improve, he began to write the long, moving, often extremely bitter letter to Douglas now known as *De Profundis*. He was not allowed to send it from prison but on his release he gave the manuscript to Robert Ross who sent a copy to Douglas and placed the original in the British Museum.

The release itself took place on 19 May 1897. After spending the morning with a few close friends, including Ada Leverson, who found him looking 'markedly better, slighter and younger than he had two years previously',

The first page of the autograph manuscript of De Profundis. *(BL Add. MS 50141A, f.1)*

The first page of a letter from Wilde written on 17 May 1897, asking his friend Reggie Turner to meet him on his release from prison. In the event, Turner was waiting for him on his arrival at Dieppe. (Private Collection)

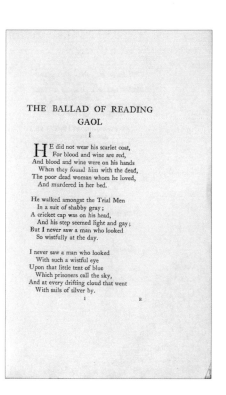

Wilde — accompanied by his friend More Adey, who had met him from prison that morning — took the afteroon train to Folkestone and the night boat to Dieppe, where Robert Ross and another old friend, Reggie Turner, were waiting for him. Once in France he adopted a new identity as Sebastian Melmoth, the surname taken from his great-uncle — Charles Maturin's Gothic novel, *Melmoth the Wanderer*. From Dieppe he moved to the small seaside town of Berneval, where he started work on his poem of suffering and betrayal, *The Ballad of Reading Gaol*, a searing indictment of man's inhumanity to man inspired by the case of Charles Wooldridge, a trooper in the Royal Horse Guards who had been hanged for the murder of his wife. It was published in February 1898, under the name 'C.3.3', Wilde's prison cell number at Reading. Constance wrote to

The title-page and first page of the first edition of The Ballad of Reading Gaol, *1898.*
(BL Ashley 4612)

her brother that it was a 'wonderful poem' but 'frightfully tragic and makes one cry'.

Although Wilde had resolved never to see Douglas again, he weakened under the bombardment of his letters and agreed – partly because he was upset at Constance's continuing refusal, on the advice of well-meaning but interfering friends, to let him see his children – to meet him in Rouen at the end of August. 'Everyone is furious with me for going back to you, but they don't understand us', he wrote afterwards. 'Do remake my ruined life for me, and then our friendship and love will have a different meaning to the world.' They arranged to spend the autumn together in Naples – a disastrous episode, as it turned out, which prompted Constance temporarily to cut off Wilde's allowance, and left him distressed, miserable and exhausted. Six months later, he wrote to Ross that he had arrived only to find that Douglas had 'no money, no plans and had forgotten all his promises', and that the reunion had been 'the most bitter experience of a bitter life'. He never saw his family again. Constance spent one last summer holiday with her sons, in the Black Forest, in 1897, before she returned to Italy and they to their separate schools in Heidelberg and Monaco. Six months later she died, following an operation on her spine. Wilde visited her grave in the cemetery at Genoa a year after her death, and was 'deeply affected – with a sense, also, of the uselessness of all regrets'. At that time, the tombstone gave only her maiden name; the words 'wife of Oscar Wilde' were not added until 1963.

The last period of Wilde's life, which he sadly declared could be 'patched up' no longer, was spent partly in Paris and partly in wandering aimlessly around Europe, with very little money, supported by a few loyal friends. 'Like dear St Francis of Assissi' he wrote, 'I am wedded to Poverty; but in my case the marriage is not a success … my thirst is for the beauty of life: my desire for the joy.' In December 1898

Frank Harris invited him to spend two months on the Riviera in the hope that he might start to write again, but the spark had gone: 'The intense energy of creation has been kicked out of me.' After some further travels in Switzerland and Italy, he returned to Paris, moving into the small and shabby Hôtel d'Alsace, whose proprietor was kind to him, and venturing out only to drink a glass of brandy or absinthe in small cafés and bars. In the autumn of 1900 a recurrent ear problem, dating back to a fall in Wandsworth prison, developed into a severe infection and an operation was carried out in his hotel room on 10 October. Complications followed and cerebral meningitis set in. Wilde was soon desperately ill, in great pain, confined to bed and intermittently delirious. Shortly before the end, Ross fulfilled his last promise to him and sent for a priest who received him into the Roman Catholic Church and administered extreme unction. He died on 30 November, not long after his forty-sixth birthday, and was given a pauper's burial in a 'sixth class' grave at Bagneux, outside the walls of Paris. It was nine years before Ross was able to move him to his present resting-place in the great cemetery of Père-Lachaise, beneath the strange and impressive tomb designed by Jacob Epstein and bearing an inscription from *The Ballad of Reading Gaol*:

Wilde's last bill from the Hôtel d'Alsace, dated 2 December 1900, two days after his death. It was paid off by Robert Ross. (Private Collection)

> *And alien tears will fill for him*
> *Pity's long broken urn*
> *For his mourners will be outcast men*
> *And outcasts always mourn.*

Further Reading

Hesketh Pearson, *The Life of Oscar Wilde* (London, 1946)

H. Montgomery Hyde, *The Trials of Oscar Wilde* (London, 1948)

Richard Ellmann, *Oscar Wilde* (London, 1987)

Peter Raby, *Oscar Wilde* (Cambridge University Press, 1988)

Merlin Holland, *The Wilde Album* (Fourth Estate, 1997)

The Complete Works of Oscar Wilde: Centenary Edition (Harper Collins, 1999)

Merlin Holland, *The Complete Letters of Oscar Wilde* (Fourth Estate, 2000)

Opposite: Wilde's final resting-place under Jacob Epstein's monument in Père-Lachaise cemetery, where his remains were transferred in 1909. (Merlin Holland)

A Wilde Chronology

1854   Oscar Wilde born in Dublin on 16 October

1871   Awarded a scholarship to Trinity College, Dublin

1874   Awarded a scholarship to Magdalen College, Oxford, where he gains a Double First in Classics in 1878

1876   Death of his father, Sir William Wilde

1879   Moves to London

1880   Writes and publishes his first play, *Vera*

1881   First edition of *Poems* published

1882   Lectures in USA and Canada all year

1883   Writes *The Duchess of Padua* in Paris; visits New York briefly for the first production of *Vera*

1884   Marries Constance Lloyd in London

1885   Moves into 16 Tite Street, Chelsea; *The Truth of Masks* published; Cyril Wilde born

1886   Meets Robert Ross, later to become his literary executor; Vyvyan Wilde born

1887   *The Canterville Ghost*, *The Sphinx without a Secret* and *The Model Millionaire* published; becomes editor of *The Woman's World*

1888   *The Happy Prince and Other Tales* and *The Young King* published

1889   *The Decay of Lying, Pen, Pencil and Poison* and *The Birthday of the Infanta* published; *The Portrait of Mr W.H.* appears in *Blackwood's Magazine*; gives up editorship of *The Woman's World*

1890   *The Picture of Dorian Gray* appears in *Lippincott's Magazine*; *The Critic as Artist* published in *The Nineteenth Century*

1891 Meets Lord Alfred Douglas; *The Duchess of Padua* produced anonymously in New York; *The Soul of Man under Socialism* published; *The Picture of Dorian Gray* published in book form; *Intentions, Lord Arthur Savile's Crime and Other Stories* and *A House of Pomegranates* published; writes *Salomé* in Paris in French

1892 *Lady Windermere's Fan* produced at the St James's Theatre; a production of *Salomé* is banned by the Lord Chamberlain

1893 *Salomé* published in French; *A Woman of No Importance* is produced at the Haymarket Theatre; *Lady Windermere's Fan* published

1894 *Salomé* published in English, with Aubrey Beardsley's illustrations; *The Sphinx, Poems in Prose* and *A Woman of No Importance* published

1895 *An Ideal Husband* produced at the Haymarket Theatre; *The Importance of Being Earnest* produced at the St James's Theatre; Wilde sues Queensberry for criminal libel; Queensberry is acquitted and Wilde is arrested for homosexual offences, tried twice, convicted and sentenced to two years' hard labour; imprisoned in Pentonville and Wandsworth before being transferred to Reading Gaol

1896 Death of his mother, Lady Wilde; *Salomé* produced in Paris

1897 Writes *De Profundis*; released from prison and crosses to France; writes and revises *The Ballad of Reading Gaol*; spends autumn with Douglas in Naples

1898 Returns to Paris; *The Ballad of Reading Gaol* published; death of Constance Wilde in Genoa; visits French Riviera with Frank Harris

1899 *The Importance of Being Earnest* and *An Ideal Husband* published; visits Switzerland and the Italian Riviera; returns to Paris and moves into Hôtel d'Alsace

1900 Travels in Italy and Sicily; returns to Paris and undergoes ear operation in hotel room; dies of cerebral meningitis on 30 November and is buried at Bagneux

Acknowledgements

This book accompanies the centenary exhibition *Oscar Wilde: A Life in Six Acts*,
on display at The British Library from 10 November 2000 to 4 February 2001 and at
the Morgan Library from 14 September 2001 to 13 January 2002. Both institutions
would like to thank all who have worked on, or assisted with, the exhibition as well as
the institutions and private collectors who have so generously lent to it: The Harry
Ransom Humanities Research Center, The University of Texas, Austin; Magdalen
College, Oxford; The National Portrait Gallery, London; The Public Record Office,
Kew; Trinity College, Dublin; The Henry W. and Albert A. Berg Collection of English
and American Literature, The New York Public Library, Astor, Lenox and Tilden
Foundations; Department of Rare Books and Special Collections, Princeton University
Library; Stephen Calloway; Sheila Colman; Roy Davids; Richard Dobbs; Mary,
Viscountess Eccles; Mr and Mrs Geoffrey Elliott; Peter Forster; Maggi Hambling;
Mark Samuels Lasner; Kimie Imura Lawlor; Jeremy Mason; Julia Rosenthal; John
Simpson; and private collectors who wish to remain anonymous. Grateful thanks are
also due to the American Trust for the British Library, Mr Rodney Leach, and the
Flemings Charitable Trust. The Morgan Library also wishes to acknowledge the
generous support of The Fay Elliott Foundation, which sponsored the New York
presentation. Finally the author would like to thank David Way and his staff in British
Library Publications, and Merlin Holland, both for the substantial loans to the
exhibition from his own family collection, and for his invaluable advice and support.